Turkey Travel Guide

Understanding Turkish Culture & Tourism

Disclaimer and Copyright Notice

Table of Contents

Introduction

Similar to Russia, Turkey is a transcontinental state (resting on more than a single continent). Its government is a republican parliamentary democracy, with the president as the chief of state and the prime minister as the head of government. Turkey's economy is a mixed one, with a burgeoning private sector coexisting with centralized economic planning and government regulation. Modern Turkish language is spoken by the natives which is the descendant of Ottoman Turkish.

Over time the language has absorbed a great many of the Arabic and Persian words. Following Turkic languages (i.e., Kazakh, Azerbaijani, Uzbek, etc.) Persian, Urdu, Arabic, a dash of French and Greek are the languages with the most shared words. Even so, communication will not be a problem with today's modern translating devices. If you're thinking about the religion, you shouldn't be concerned because Turkey is a secular country with a majority of Muslim population. They are really friendly and open-minded people who will greet you regardless of your beliefs.

Ankara, originally known as Angora, is Turkey's capital and is located in the northwest of the country. Approximately 125 km south of the stunning Black Sea. In 333 BCE, Alexander the Great seized this city but from 1356 it has been under Muslim rule. The city's existing architecture reflects its diverse history.

Turkey has grown to prominence as one of the world's most visited countries in recent years, thanks in part to the beauty of its cities, particularly Constantinople, now known as Istanbul, the Republic of Turkey's primary city, seaport, and financial center. It is a cultural and historical center. It is still a bustling metropolis. A favored place to visit by tourists when they plan a trip to this country.

The Sultan Ahmet Cami (Blue Mosque) right in the heart of Istanbul

Everything is very riveting, from the beauty of the people to the land itself. That being said, everything has its pros and cons. While they might be the kindest people a little awareness is still needed. Be conscious of scams or pick pockets. Take care of your valuables. Don't trust just anyone!

Chapter 1: Turkey For Foreigners

Turkey is strategically placed near the Turkish Straits, which connect the Black and Aegean Seas. The geography in the west is made up of narrow coastal plains that become rockier as you travel east. Neighboring by several European and Asian countries; Bulgaria to the north and a bit to the northeast, Georgia. From the west there is Greece. Armenia, Azerbaijan, and Iran are to its east. Syria lies to the south, and Iraq is to the southeast. On the terrain, there are various high mountains. On the Armenian-Iranian border, Mount Ararat, Armenia's highest mountain, rises to 16,945 feet. Don't worry about the supper you just ate; the terrain is steep across the country, so you'll get plenty of exercise!

There are four primary elevations in the western section. Some are narrower, steeper, and have slopes, while others are tall and have slopes. The famed Bosphorus passage connects the Black Sea with the Marmara Sea. It is a flooded valley that does not follow a straight path but rather follows an abrupt direction to the Southeast and Northwest. It's around 32 kilometers long and 120 meters deep. It's a natural waterway that's used for international trade.

Many commercial ships and oil tankers, as well as local fishing and passenger boats, use this channel. Possible dangers of the swirls in the strait can hinder many a new inexperienced fellow who travel through it. To connect the two sides of Bosphorus, there are a total of three bridges over the strait. These are all suspension bridges and present a marvelous view when seen from either side. In fact, the view is just amazing from atop the bridge as well. A system for travelling (connecting dual continents) is propped up under sea with two long well-built and lighted tunnels.

15 percent of Turkey's mass is covered by the Mediterranean Sea. But the great thing about the land that it adjoins is that it is ideal for growing citrus fruits, rice, cereals, cotton and other essential

industrial products like wheat, barley, aluminum, steel etc. The region contains plains with enriched agricultural soils combined with a suitable weather. A lot of the growth of oranges and mandarins takes place in this area along with bananas. The rivers rise during spring when snow is melting and the weather can get harsh with dry & droughty summer times.

1.1 Turkey's climate

Due to the hills and beaches, Turkey offers a diverse range of shifting climates that vary from area to location. Even the day and night climates don't match. A microclimate condition in one place may be quite different from that in another. Because of the sea breezes, the weather at the shore is cool and windy most of the time. Inside the land, the weather is radically different. Winters bring cold flurries and temperatures as low as 0 degrees, while summers can bring burning daytimes along with cool nights. Summer days are made even better by this weather combination.

In the same location, you may enjoy both types of weather because a large variety of foods can each have their own appeal. Cold drinks, slushes', cold beverages, street delicacies like mussels, ice creams, and fresh cold sliced fruits like watermelon, pomegranate in a glass, or oranges can be a fantastic joy from early morning to late afternoon. Since it gets a little colder in the evenings, hot items such as soups, bakery goods, coffees, and freshly baked pies can all be enjoyed. There is a special drink which is highly consumed by Turkish people before, after meals or over a conversation, called Çay which is basically a tea.

Vacationers are in high number throughout the summer season, which spans from the end of May to the end of September so it is not best to go then if you want tranquility. The best periods to visit are late spring (April to May) and early fall (September to early October). Winters stick around for a lot longer, with snow on the ground from November until the end of April. As a result, it's a terrific time to see snow fall. Spring and fall have moderate weather, however there might be a quick change in these in some locations.

1.2 Turkish locals

When you think about Turkish people, you think of people who are outgoing, expressive, kind, and welcoming. This can be said about them by anyone who has encountered them. If they are content, they will ensure that everyone around them is content as well. When you stay at a hotel, they will do everything they can to make you feel welcome. These people place a high value on their relationships with friends and family. They exhibit love to children and esteem and respect their elders. Their culture and customs are very important to them, but they also like partying and having a good time. Even their seniors will dance at their weddings. Turkish people are extremely proud of their heritage and are eager to share their history and culture with guests. People will be more than happy to give you stories about their hometown's history while showing you the attractions no matter where you travel.

They are enamored with romance and love which can be seen in their songs, dramas and beliefs. As a result, they value friendships. If there is an open event of some kind, they will occasionally form groups to dance in the street, and others are welcome to participate. In the cities, light cultural instrumental music is frequently heard. If you're sitting by the seashore, music will make the experience much more worthwhile. Shopping in the local bazaars can also be a lot of fun because the locals love to barter, so don't be hesitant and take advantage of it.

One thing to keep in mind is that people in rural areas speak English far less fluently than those in urban areas. When visiting such locations, hire a translator, a guide, or bring a competent translator app on your phone. In most cases, they will be quite useful in making a dialogue with just expressions alone in markets, but as a general rule, a translation tool will be very useful. Don't be scared to ask strangers for directions if you get lost. They will genuinely strive to assist you and may even invite you over for a cup of tea afterwards.

Many individuals there have a soft spot for cats and dogs. They love animals and treat them well, so be careful not to offend them, especially cats. Don't stomp on them, throw things at them, or bully them. Kind Turkish folk provide them with their own homes, feed them, and look after them. They can be found all across the country. The pets' natures have developed to be nice to people since they are properly fed and loved. As a result, any animals present are likely to become attached fast.

Shelters and road signs for animals

Other religions' events are appreciated and celebrated throughout the year, in addition to their own cultural traditions. Because there is such a large Muslim population, the Islamic month of Ramadan is celebrated. In Turkey, the Ramadan Feast (Eid-ul-Fitr) is an official holiday that lasts three days. During this time, government buildings, schools, and most businesses are closed. Eid-ul-Adha is another popular celebration.

Because only 2 percent of the Turkish population is Christian, they don't truly celebrate Christmas on December 25th, but the streets are decked out in lights and other festive decorations. Those who are celebrating have their homes beautifully decorated or will go to Christmas services at their churches. New Year's Eve is a considerably larger celebration that is celebrated throughout Turkey. Families and friends gather to commemorate this happy event and they normally have a huge feast with a roasted turkey as the main course. They play games and party and as the clock strikes 12, everyone yells out 'Yeni Yılın Kutlu Olsun!' (Meaning 'Happy New Year').

1.3 Cultural treasures of Turkey

Our lives are spiced up by customs and traditions, which make us feel good. They contribute to the formation of our national identity. They provide us happiness and give us hope. They bring families together when they are celebrated, and we realize how amazing our traditions are when we tell others about them. Turkish people adore and are proud of their heritage and cultures. The prominent ones have been mentioned here.

Turkish coffee is well-known for its delectable aroma. The Turks drink at least one cup of coffee per day, and occasionally more. They do a really unique thing where they leave a little coffee in the cup after they've finished drinking it and let it cool down before telling the future with the rest of the coffee. That is their method of foretelling the future!

Another prevalent belief is the 'Evil eye,' which is said to protect against bad luck. It's a glass stone with a blue painted eye on the inside and a blue white painted outside. Necklaces, bracelets, anklets, and fridge magnets come in a variety of forms and sizes. It can be hung anyplace to keep negativity at bay. This is Turkey's most famous souvenir, which can be found in any shop. Its Turkish name is Nazar Boncugu.

If you've seen people with cups in their hands at train stations, it's because they're spraying a little water on the departing passengers as a sign of wishing good luck on their travels.

Another amusing practice is for the bride to write the names of all the single women in her circle of friends and family under her shoes; if the name remains, it is bad luck and you will not be marrying anytime soon; if the name goes, it is a sign you will be tying the knot soon!

Hidrellez is a non-religious holiday in Turkey that commemorates the beginning of spring when the prophets Hydir and Ilyas met on this world on the night of May 5th. The idea is to write a wish on a piece of paper (others prefer a stone) and bury it beneath the rose plant soil in the evening. A fire is built afterwards. The locals take turns jumping over it. The next morning before sunrise, they pick up the paper or rock and throw it in the river, burn it, or leave it under the earth. It gives people optimism that their dreams and wishes will become true soon. A wish tree, similar to this custom, is a tree on which a colorful thread of cloth is hung, and while doing so, you must think of your wish, which will be granted.

These people like to give their children names that are inspired by nature e.g., the name Alev which means Flame, Altan or Red Dawn, Ayberk meaning High Moon, Bahar literally the Spring Season or Gunduz meaning Daytime.

The Hagia Sophia Holy Grand Mosque in Istanbul is one of Turkey's most well-known tourist attractions. It has a long and illustrious history. The mosque's exquisite baby pink and sky-blue colors which are a stunning sight to behold. The mosque's architecture and mosaics are examples of the country's rich cultural heritage. The Sultan Ahmet Cami (Blue Mosque) is located in the center of Istanbul. The blue tiles, as the name implies, cover the mosque's inner walls. The mosque is open to the public, however non-believers are not permitted to enter during the five daily prayer periods. Don't be fooled by someone who promises to take you there quickly because they will simply try to sell you items at their shops while you wait in line to enter the mosque with other tourists from the south door rather than the entrance.

The best time to visit this mosque is in the evening, when it is quieter and less crowded. And be sure to put your shoes in the plastic bags provided at the entrance and cover appropriately before going in as it is a holy place.

The Topkapi Palace in Istanbul's Fatih neighborhood is one of Turkey's most famous and beautiful museums. The Sulemaniye Mosque is a well-known skyline feature in Istanbul. The artistically decorated tombs of Sultan Süleyman I and his wife Haseki Hürrem Sultan can also be found on the mosque grounds.

Outside of Istanbul, an important monument to see is Bursa's 600-year-old Grand Mosque, which is located in the city's heart.

Perhaps the most archeologically important is the Greek city of Ephesus, which is located in the current hamlet of Selcuk in Turkey. The structures depict how the Romans lived in the past. It truly takes one's breath away. Many historians think that Saint John composed his Gospel in Ephesus, and that after the Virgin Mary died, he brought her to the lush hills of Selcuk, above Ephesus, and lay her to rest there. These structures in the current village demonstrate how structures have changed over time. The great theatre of ancient Ephesus is a must-see attraction. And there's the old Celsius library.

1.4 Turkey's landmarks and their rich history

Turkey is a country steeped in ancient history, from Greek dominance through Roman and Lycian rule coming to the Great Ottomans, all of whom greatly prized the country for its natural beauty. So, of course there are many amazing places to see. The top 5 famous and must-see landscapes around the country include:

❖ Lake Van

Lake Van, with its enticing blue waters, rests near the Iranian border in eastern Anatolia. Sometimes referred to as the Sea of Van, being the country's largest lake. The unique significance it has is because of Mount Ararat, Turkey's tallest peak on top of being a volcanic cone and one of numerous mountains that surround it. Before being drowned in water, it had a full town buried underneath. The remains of the Altinsac Church are another attraction on the lake that you get along with the breathtaking vistas.

❖ The Blue Lagoon

A beach side community is another beauty to witness in the province of Mugla, Fethiye city. Several luxury hotels, private beaches, and water activities are sprinkled around the blue lagoon, acclaimed for its ever-changing vibrant turquoise and azure shades. It is among the premier paragliding spot across the nation, if you're in the mood to spend some days unleashing your adventurous spirit. You also have the option to indulge in swimming in the seas, and if you're lucky, you might see some turtles.

❖ Mediterranean Sea

Summer is usually a great time to visit the islands, and if you're a beach lover, a sun queen, or an ocean dreamer, how about cruising on a yacht? Then look no farther than the Mediterranean Sea in Fethiye city, which offers an incredible selection of charter boats to rent, including both motor (power) yachts and sailing yachts, as well as the increasingly popular huge luxury private super yacht rentals. Local cuisine, which is served on these ships, speaks much about a country's traditions. Of course, the menu is not fixed and can be varied if requested beforehand. Everything is prepared from scratch, and you are welcome to enjoy snacks you bring along.

During summer, freshly cut bright fruits are a treat. Any dietary or special preferences for a favorite wine or dish will also be taken in account in advance.

A perfect vacation spot on the Mediterranean Sea

❖ Cappadocia

Cappadocia is a region that is positioned quite in the center of Turkey. It houses few of the country's strangest sights, such as fairy chimneys, Bronze Age cave houses, and stone-built churches. Every sunset changes the color of this strange scene of carved-out towering rock formations. The story behind these stone outcroppings is fascinating. Volcanic eruptions in the past transformed the area into ash, which settled into soft sand. Persecuted Christians escaped here in Roman times and constructed their homes in these caves. A stay inside the caves can also be arranged for tourists. This is a completely unique experience. Traditional Turkish cuisine is accessible.

Hot air balloons in Cappadocia

Apart from these historical aspects, those who appreciate flying and seeing something different will enjoy Cappadocia owing to the remarkable rock formations. Hot air balloons aren't just a sight to behold, but they can also be ridden. These polka-dotted hot air balloons in the sky form a grand attraction of this place. Most of them take off from the Goreme national park a UNESCO approved world heritage site.

❖ Pamukkale

Pamukkale (aka the 'Cotton Sky') is a natural beauty towards the west of Turkey. The pristine mineral rich thermal sky-blue waters flowing down white travertine terraces look mesmerizing. This place was actually used by the Romans as a spa. It has a magnificent theatre as well as a tomb-filled necropolis. It combines both natural and man-made marvels. It is possible to stroll up or down the terrace ridge stretching from Pamukkale hamlet to the central entrance to the Hierapolis ancient site on the summit. Only this section of the travertines can be walked on, and it must be done barefoot.

The wonderful Pamukkale

Chapter 2: Travel Planning; Living, Eating And Getting Around

The Turkish lira is the official currency. Exchange rate of Lira is cheaper for most European currencies and the dollar. The country has relaxed travel restrictions and for some nations there is visa-on-arrival. For those that do need approval beforehand, getting a visa is not a big issue. The only thing that could go wrong, resulting in rejection is the possibility that you didn't fill in the info right so ensure correctness of details before submitting.

For thoroughly exploring a place, even a month seems inadequate to grasp the true essence. So, it might not be possible to cover the abundant scenic views and activities that amazing Turkey has to offer but this book will suggest the best places to cover and make your trip worthwhile in just as little as a couple of weeks! In two weeks, a lot may be ticked off your Turkey Travel bucket list with planning done right.

The finest times to visit are from the periods of April/May (spring) or September/October with fewer crowds all around the country. It would be a bad idea to go in June, July or August since it is really hot with peak tourist season and with much higher prices. Skiing season begins November to March so a lot to see and do during these months.

2.1 Bookings, cost cutting solutions and what to pack

Setting a budget is a crucial step when planning any trip. And travelling to this place as a budget traveler who does not want to break the bank is totally doable.

Have some dollars saved ahead of your journey and be sure to have some Liras with you before going there in case of emergencies. Don't convert money in the exchanges at the airport because it will cost a lot (same goes for SIM cards), do so once you're out in the city area. Book your travel tickets ahead of time, both for travel into Turkey and around the country for cheaper tickets via online sites. There are many sites that offer discounts on one-two week trips with return ticket and much can be saved by pre-bookings.

When it comes to hotels, a neat hack during off-season is to check out prices on booking sites for the duration of your stay and then book for the first night only. Once you're in the city, check out the hotels you narrowed down on the website and approach them directly for booking the rest of your stay. They will offer lower prices for sure because now they don't have to pay the websites commission and neither do you! Although a bit expensive but hotels/hostels closer to the markets will be worthwhile in terms of time and bus fare savings.

If you are a history and architecture buff, you will want to check out the myriad of museums across Turkey. The Ministry of Culture and Tourism has made it easy to save on entrance tickets by introducing a Museum Pass which, once purchased, gives you free access for 15 days to all the sites run by the department.

Some travel essentials; a travel guide/map, sunscreen is a must for protection against tanning or sun burns, a hat/cap or an umbrella for sunny weather, of course a camera for the pictures, a hand carry for personal instant things, an adapter because the plug types found in Turkey are C or F so you will definitely want one for plugging your appliances into wall sockets, a swimsuit if the hotel has a pool and possibly a scarf will come handy for breezy evenings or when modesty is required for entering any areas. The clothing's depend on the season you choose to go in but you will definitely need comfortable walking shoes for the steep terrain around the country.

2.2 Food hubs, fancy dining & nightlife

Among the best of the best comes Turkish cuisine rich in vegetables, meat and smothered in olive oil. The food is so delightful whilst being healthy. Everything is cooked to perfection. They have these really sweet sayings before enjoying any meals 'afiyet olsun' which means enjoy your meal and 'ellerinize sağlık' meaning health to your hands. Food carts on the streets have hot selling iconic simits (a kind of bagel bread), kumpir, kofte ekmek, doner, gozleme, pulav or a snack as simple as roasted chickpeas that go by the name 'leblebi' and many more things. The country is famous for its kebabs so do try them. There are many eggplant based dishes to try from as well.

The meme sensation of 2017, the very famous butcher and food entertainer Nusret Gökçe recognized by Salt Bae also resides in Turkey and the steak houses Nusr-et that he owns are in Istanbul. His unique style of preparing and seasoning the delicious thick and juicy steak is unmatched. The restaurants are little pricey but worth it for dinner and show.

Having a larger Muslim majority, Turkey offers a great list of halal foods but since it is also a secular country, alcohol is also widely available along with thriving clubs, partying, DJs, live music and much more in the night life. Ritim, Nardis Jazz Club and Escape club Istanbul are few famous ones to show you a good partying time. Vigneron Wine House in Istanbul and Alp's Wine house in Antalya are both good for excellent wine and fine dining. Visit other restaurants near the sea that provide a beautiful view.

2.3 Top 4 Turkish cities to visit & explore

❖ Istanbul

The majority of travelers prefer to live in Sultanahmet (the old city) or the Taksim district. The Istanbul card operates a comprehensive, clean, and tourist-friendly public transportation system that includes not only the city metro but also buses, ferries, and cable cars. Using boats, day visits to Princes' Island and Bursa are possible from Istanbul. The iconic Turkish breakfast, iskendar kebab, and pide bread are must-tries, but don't miss out on cart cuisine like borek (similar to a cheese patty), kumpir (stuffed potato), and roasted chestnuts, to mention a few. Famous sites to see are the Bosphorus, Topkapi and Dolmabase Palace, Aya Sofia Cami, Sultan Ahmet Cami, Galata Tower, Grand Bazar and Spice Bazar.

❖ Ankara

There are many monuments and museums dedicated to Ataturk in Turkey's capital. The high-speed train takes roughly 4-5 hours to get from Istanbul to Ankara and is a delightful mid-range alternative. When booked in advance, in-country air travel with local carriers is rather inexpensive. Kizilay is located in the heart of the city, with easy access to all of the city's major attractions.

❖ Bursa

Bursa, Turkey's fourth largest city, is worth a day journey
from Istanbul. There, Mount Uludag is a home to Turkey's
popular ski resorts. Taking a ship from Istanbul is the coolest,
although it's not always doable when it's raining. The city
is also known for hot springs and thermal spas, the best of
which are run by hotels. The koza han is considered the oldest
covered market on the route of the infamous Silk Route.

❖ Izmir

Izmir has a really charming feel, owing to its proximity to open water and a relaxed atmosphere found to be lacking in Istanbul. The city itself offers plenty sights worth seeing such as the Saat Kuhlesi (or Clock Tower) as well as the promenade. However, at a manageable distance from the city and worthy of a day trip, there are excursions worth undertaking, such as Pamukkale (Denizli) and Selcuk to behold what was once the Roman empire and its town of Ephesus as mentioned earlier. Both are World Heritage sites recognized by UNESCO. Izmir does not have a comprehensive tram system; however, buses traverse all the routes. It suffered a major earthquake in October 2020 however, most tourist spots were unaffected.

2.4 Luscious landscapes and getting around

The list of UNESCO sites with World Heritage status does not end at the magnificent Pamukkale and Ephesus. Pergamon and Asclepion are renowned as the birthplace of parchment paper along with the earliest therapeutic hubs on the globe.

Gobeklitepe, the historical zero point, is sure to fascinate. The owner, Mr. Mahmut Yildiz is always more than happy to talk to tourists.

Atalhöyük is one more remarkable spot and is, to-date, believed to be the pioneer village/town in human history. It put the foundation for urban centers today.

Hattusa, the heart of the Hattire Empire and Ani's ruins, that include approximately 1000 churches are all rather inspiring.

Aphrodisias is the primeval city of Aphrodite, the goddess of love and beauty.

The country's section belonging to the Black Sea, with its opulent sceneries, is a great place to disconnect and get lost in nature's bounty and man-made retreats. Sumela Monastery is a well-known tourist attraction near the Black Sea.

Public transport is a very economical method to make your way within the city. The Istanbulkart, applicable to the city of Istanbul, has great value for money when getting around the city. It applies to a great many transport options like ferry, nostalgic tram, funicular, and cable cars. However, these may be out of bounds or inaccessible for some people, so calling an uber to your door front using the Bitaksi app is another great option. Taxis, on the other hand, will be significantly pricier, so utilize public transportation including dolmuş (minibuses). Or, if you're a young or fit person, rent a bicycle.

When flying to your destination, it is worth remembering that Sabiha Gokcen Airport (SAW) on the Asian part is roughly 40 kilometers from the city center, and Istanbul Airport (IST) is located on the European side, approximately 50 kilometers from the city center. More alternative for getting from one city to the next is to take a shuttle bus or go via high speed or regular train.

As a country surrounded by lots of water, ferries are commonplace and inexpensive mode of transportation. Can't complain if they are also the most enjoyable and picturesque!

2.5 Health and safety precautions

Although the top cities to visit mentioned above are quite safe, you can travel to Turkey alone, as a man or woman, as long as you take basic safety precautions.

First of all, tourists must have health insurance, and they must arrange their travels through a reputable website. Avoid the Syrian border and nearer places for safety purposes.

When entering the holy magnificent mosques, men should wear slacks that cover their legs and women should wear a few clothing that cover their legs and heads.

Parents travelling with children should bring a stroller because the roads are uphill and can be tiresome, as well as a carry cot because certain streets lack pavements, tissues because they aren't readily available in every bathroom, and some public facilities charge a fee, usually 1 Turkish lira. Keep a watch on your child at all times to avoid becoming lost, as well as while allowing it to pet dogs or other animals, as some may be dangerous.

Maintain a low profile and wear minimal jewelry to reduce your chances of being robbed or conned. Summer temperatures are particularly hot, so wear sunscreen, carry a water bottle with you at all times since the tap water could cause problems and isn't of good taste. Avoid religious and political inconsistencies. Before visiting a monument, read the warning labels to see if photography is permitted. To avoid getting lost, write down the name and address of your hotel on a piece of paper. Particularly in touristy places, take care of valuables or carry an anti-theft gadget. Alcohol drinking while driving will result in a fine and a six-month license suspension. Be cautious and avoid venturing out late at night.

2.6 Shopping & souvenirs

❖ The Grand Bazaar

A world acclaimed shopping arena that gets some of the most tourist footfall in the world, the Grand Bazar is a labyrinth of 60 plus streets and countless arteries running through it. There are thousands of stores housed within alongside banks, its own praying spaces, eateries, police station and even a dedicated post office!

This is where you may find some of Turkey's top handicrafts and souvenirs. Traditional jewelry, carpets off of traditional hand looms popularly called kilims, lanterns/lamps, ceramics, Turkish metal ware specially nargile, a sort of pipe used for smoking tobacco, other small textiles like cushions or pillows, edible delights for gifts or yourself (although you should probably save this for the famous spice bazaar).

The Grand Bazaar

Some handy tips; you cannot cover the whole bazaar in just one day so plan ahead, go early in the morning, the bazaar opens at about 8:30 am in the morning and closes till 7:00 pm or dedicate two days at least to this place because there is a whole town waiting to be discovered here. Offering tea is part and parcel of Turkish hospitality and will be offered at every shop here so indulge in tea with the shopkeepers as you chat and haggle, making the most of it. They may take advantage of your being from out of town and jack up prices accordingly so don't purchase anything without going through at least a few shops first. Then branch away from the main streets to explore hidden gems and exhilarating bargains.

Souvenirs and delights in the Grand Bazar

❖ **The Spice Bazaar**

An Egyptian market in Istanbul, the Spice Bazar is near the Galata Bridge, and the Sulemaniye Mosque in the Fatih district's Eminonu area. You can take the tram from Sultanahmet to this location, although walking is more enjoyable. Well-versed with the locals. this is a smaller version of the Grand Bazar, with less aggressive vendors and lower pricing. However, the gated section closes in the evening, so go early. Turkish delicacies, tea leaves, cheese, various local nuts, dried fruits, saffron, and, of course, spices will all be found in this traditional spice market shop. After a few hours of wandering, stop by the Mado dondurma shop to enjoy some tasty ice cream, or if you're hungry, a variety of teas and delicious sandwiches are also available. The coffee shop 'Mehmet Efendi' is well-known for their traditional Turkish roasted coffee beans. When in Istanbul and seeking experience that will engage all of your senses, the Spice Bazaar should not be skipped.

Chapter 3: Reasons To Go

In the many pros of visiting turkey, for every age group, there are different attractions and charms. The burgeoning art scene, which provides free exhibitions for formal events. In Turkey, no view is unattractive. Every location you visit will have its own unique style and activities. Boredom has no place on our journey. Now is the time to finally start making plans for that long-awaited trip to Turkey on your bucket list.

3.1 Family getaway during kids' vacations

As mentioned above, this nation has something to offer to everyone and that includes kids and teenagers as well.

❖ **The Lego Land Theme Park**

Istanbul is home to the Lego Land theme park. A lego-themed playground with play zones, thrilling rides, and a 4D theatre built right inside the park. Easily accessible via public transportation.

❖ **Basilica Cistern**

The Basilica Cistern, like the other cisterns, is an underground location where water is stored for various reasons, as it was in ancient times, but this one supplied the Great Palace. It will appeal to your adolescent audience. It has two column bases with medusa heads. The origins of the two heads are uncertain, however they are likely to have been transferred to the cistern after being taken from a late Roman edifice. This location has also been used as the backdrop for a James Bond film.

Medusa head (right) in the Basilica Cistern (left)

❖ Miniaturk Park

Miniaturk Park is an amusement park in Istanbul. There are around 105 tiny cute models of different places of the country in this park. The miniatures are built perfectly matching to the places. The majority hail from Istanbul, with the remainder hailing from Anatolia and Ottoman regions of Turkey.

3.2 Honeymoon destination

Turkey has risen to prominence on the world map in recent years, and as a result, it has become the most popular destination for newlyweds, owing to its romantic landscapes, exciting adventures, relaxing vacation time, abundance of things to do with your partner, moonlight boat rides, and excellent and unique cuisines. There's so much buried treasure here that it's ideal for a couple's vacation. For their honey mooning customers, the hotel management goes to great lengths to deliver an amazing experience. Some hotels even place sweets and fruit baskets on the table and finish making the bed with swan-shaped towels and flower petals.

❖ **Prince's Island**

The Prince's Island is located away from the hustle and bustle of Istanbul's daily life. Enjoy a 90-minute ferry voyage to Buyukada with views of Kiz Kulesi and Topkapi Palace, walk about and explore the island, stay for a day, ride a bike or horse-drawn carriages around the area, and book a hotel with a pool for breakfast and have a fun ride back.

Mesmerizing vistas in the Prince's Island

❖ Marmaris

Visit this hotspot for a more interesting and wild evening near the shore. It's jam-packed with activities. In a yacht, sail along the coast. Explore the castle in Marmaris. Take a day excursion to Rhodes, a Greek island. Take a walk along the Bay's beach. Along the Daylan River, take a cruise. Take a trip of the Datca Peninsula in a jeep.

3.3 Travel with friends or solo

Traveling alone can be amazing, but it's much better when you have company. There's a lot of fun and adventures to be had with friends and family. Specially in sports like skiing, paragliding or scuba diving. Because diving is a perilous sport, new divers are put to the test in small pools to practice their skills before venturing into the real world. Another water adventure is white water rafting on the Koprulu and Antaria rivers. Climbing, mountaineering, jumping, abseiling, and surfing over waterfalls, as well as windsurfing and kiteboarding, are becoming increasingly popular in Turkey.

Conclusion

This riveting Turkey travel guide with its tomes of information and tips and hacks will provide you with all of the necessary details, from the greatest sites to visit to the ideal ways to conduct yourself in the nation. It will show you how to get around and adjust to the local culture and have an unforgettable adventure that you'll be sharing with friends and relatives for ages to come.

İyi şanslar ve iyi yolculuklar! (Good luck and happy travels!)

Printed in Great Britain
by Amazon

85718900R00023